LIFE AS A ROLLERCOASTER

Have No fear, Just Enjoy it

By: Daphia Jones Hicks

SOUTHERN WOMEN PUBLISHING

www.southernwomenstories.com

This book is dedicated to my brothers and sisters in Christ. I want to give a special dedication to my beloved family: Husband; Dominique Hicks, Son; Drayson Hicks, Mother; Anna Jones, Father; James Jones, Sisters; Latonya Robertson and LaDonna Jones, Niece; Regilyn Robertson, Mother in Law; Shirley Hicks, and Sister in law; Shawntina Hicks. I want to give a special thanks to those that were on this book-writing journey with me as they too published their book the same day: LaMonique Mac, Laqueisha Price, Leanita Crawford Hunt, and Bishop John Hunt. All of us are embarking on a rollercoaster journey. I pray that this book gives us the courage to face all of life's challenges without fear.

CONTENTS

CHAPTER 1: UPS

* * *

The ups that we experience in life refer to the good days and the good times. It is times when everything is well. You are enjoying your time here on this Earth. Everyone loves the ups season, you may find yourself saying, "Life is great" or "I love my life". I have witnessed myself saying that I am in a "good place" in life. "A good place" means that a person is doing well and is satisfied with life. Emotionally you are calm and at peace. You find yourself smiling a lot more. You are content with everything and life couldn't be any better. The sun is constantly shining, birds are singing, butterflies are swarming, and flowers are blooming. Now let's elaborate on the ups that we experience in life.

Ups refer to accomplishments. When you have accomplished something that has been a challenge, it makes you feel fantastic. What were your thoughts when you graduated from high school? After being in school for at least 13 years, you are proud of yourself. Some of your other accomplishments may include: getting accepted into college, graduating from college, getting married, buying a home, starting a family, etc. It is a proud moment for not only you to experience, but for you to see other people experience.

Ups refer to promotions. Everyone loves "going up", meaning achieving and obtaining more. It feels great to be promoted. To be promoted means to go to the next level. When you get promoted to a higher position on your job, most times you get a raise in pay. Who does not love raises and bonuses? There are many people that start from the bottom and work themselves up. It feels great to experience each level of increase. God allows these doors to open. God is the one that blesses us with these great opportunities. We should not take these moments for granted.

Ups refer to positivity in your life. You have a positive attitude. The people around you have a positive attitude. You are building friendships. Your relationships/marriages are thriving. You are not fighting with your partner or spouse. You are "happy" with one another. You wake up happy. You don't find yourself "waking up on the wrong side of the bed" often. You are excited to start your day. There is so much positivity in your life that your mind is clear, and you can rationalize your thoughts. Your mind is not crowded. You are more creative and your days are more productive.

Ups refer to a season that God has answered your prayers. Everything you have prayed for has come into existence. When God answers your prayers, it feels like a weight has been lifted. You do not feel like you are drowning and suffocating in burdens. You feel excited and relieved. You are thankful to God that He has heard your prayers and that things are working in your favor. You are experiencing blessings after blessings. God has come to your rescue on time. You are feeling so liberated and free.

Ups refer to being financially stable. You are not in lack when it comes to finances. All of your bills are paid in full and on time each month. You have plenty of food in your home. You have money left to take care of your wants. You are traveling several times throughout the year. You are living your best life. You do not have to live on a strict budget. You can bless others and give freely to those in need.

✳ ✳ ✳

Dear Heavenly Father, in the mighty name of Jesus, I come be-

fore you in prayer for the reader and their family. Lord, I pray for the continuous blessings in the lives of your people in the Spirit and in the natural. Lord, I pray that your favor is upon them and their family. Lord, I pray that your people are continuously thanking you for everything that they have. Lord, I thank you for what you have done, what you are doing, and what you will do in the future. I pray that your people never take anything that you do for granted. Lord, we know that you give, and you also take away. Lord, I pray that your people will be grateful. I pray that your people will be cheerful givers. Lord, I pray that you continue to give your people perfect peace. Lord, I pray that your people will continue to prosper. In Jesus name, we pray. Amen.

CHAPTER 2: DOWNS

* * *

The down season that we experience in life refers to the bad days and the bad times. It is when you find yourself in bad situations. It is usually filled with sadness, pain, and disappointments. The down season is when it rains in your life, and it seems like the sun is never going to shine. The down season is when one bad thing happens after the other. Many people are familiar with the phrase, "You cannot win for losing". The down season is when you endure loses. It seems like you cannot catch a break. Every time you look up, disappointment strikes. Now let's elaborate on the downs we experience in life.

Downs refer to hardships. Hardships are times when you experience famine. You are experiencing a financial drought. You are having a hard time making ends meet. You do not know how a certain bill is going to get paid. You do not know where your next meal is going to come from. You are temporarily unemployed.

You are putting in applications, but you are not getting a response. You need a car, but your lack of income and low credit score prohibits you from getting one. You have to catch rides with whoever is willing to give you a ride. Those people get tired of transporting you because you cannot afford to supply them with gas money. You want to give gas money, but you simply do not have it to give. You cannot afford a cab, UBER, or even the city bus. You find yourself walking to the majority of places that you need to go. You have small children. They get really tired of having to walk several miles to the grocery store with you, but they are too young to stay home. Your children shoes wear out quickly from so much walking, but you cannot afford to buy them a new pair. You do not have a lot of family support to call on for help. You see the effect of your children getting teased in school because their clothes and shoes are worn out. Your sons cannot get their haircuts as needed because you cannot afford it.

Downs refer to failing relationships and marriages. We all know it hurts to separate from someone we love so dearly. The first choice should always be to fight spiritually for your relationship/marriage. The more you fight to stay, it seems like the worse everything gets. You are being physically, mentally, verbally, and emotionally abused. You are torn and do not know what to do. You have children with this person. The children are witnessing the fights and arguments. You find yourself crying yourself to sleep many nights because you are so unhappy. You do not have anyone to talk to that understands. Your friends and family are done hearing about it because they told you to leave, but you keep going back.

Downs refer to addictions. You have been through an extensive amount of pain in your life. You have turned to an excessive use of drugs and alcohol to cope with the trauma you've experienced. You cannot miss a day from drinking alcohol or using drugs. The pain you have been through is so overbearing that you even tried to overdose yourself. You have been in mental health facilities for anxiety and depression. You have been to too many rehabs. You always relapse every time you go back into that same environment with other users. You have been called, "crazy and useless". You spend all of your money on drugs and alcohol. You do not have your own house or a car. You are constantly in and out of residents. Also, you have been in and out of jail for drug possessions and DUI's. Your children have been placed in foster care due to lack of stability and neglect. You love your children, but this addiction has a stronghold on you.

Downs refer to deaths in our lives. The loss of a family member or friend by death is never easy. It is even harder if they died in a tragedy because it leaves you with so many questions. You may not have had the opportunity to say good-bye. You wish you never would have had an argument as your last conversation. You wish you would have spent more time with them. You wish you would have had the chance to apologize for anything you've done wrong.

* * *

Dear Heavenly Father, in the mighty name of Jesus, I come before you in prayer for the reader and their family. Lord, bless them in their time of need. Bless their home and their family. Lord, I know that you will supply their every need according to your riches in glory. I pray that your people seek you first, and you will add all things unto them. I come against the spirit of lack. Your people will live in abundance. They will have more than enough. I bind the spirit of addiction. Your people will be delivered from drugs and alcohol. I pray that we all seek a spiritual high. Lord, we want to be drunk in the Holy Spirit (Ephesians 5:18). I pray that you give us peace in our homes. Lord, I pray that you restore families and marriages. In Jesus name, we pray. Amen.

CHAPTER 3: TWIST AND TURNS

✽ ✽ ✽

The twists and turns season that we experience in life refers to the different paths that life takes you on. It is never a straight road. Have you ever been watching a movie and you had the ending mapped out in your head? When you actually saw the ending, it was something totally unexpected. It is when you do not see something coming. It is the unpredictable outcomes of life. It is the things you would never plan for yourself. Now let's elaborate on the twists and turns that we experience in life.

Twists and turns refer to an unexpected illness. You are as healthy as can be. The next thing you know you find out you have a terminal illness. You are so afraid. Everyone tells you it is going to be okay, but you just don't see it to be true. You are losing weight. You are losing all of your hair. You cannot keep any food down. You have children that you want to live for. You are fighting hard, but you keep getting weaker and weaker. You spend more days in the hospital than at home. All you can think about is your children and how you have to beat this illness for them.

Twists and turns refer to unexpected deaths. A mother carries her child full term. The pregnancy was wonderful. The day of the delivery the doctor announces the child is stillborn. She never thought this would happen to her. Every doctor's appointment went well. There were no risks. She is so confused and heartbroken.

Twists and turns refer to car accidents. One minute you are driving down the road, the next minute you are in a fatal car accident. Car accidents are deadly. It is by the grace of God when people make it out alive. Some people make it out with minor injuries. On the other hand, some people become seriously injured. Some injuries can take months to heal. Some injuries cause your body to never function the same.

Twist and turns refer to burglaries. Each burglary is different. Some burglaries happen with no physical harm. However, it harms you mentally when you don't feel safe in your home. The things you have worked hard for are now stolen and/or damaged. Some victims see the robber face-to-face. This has to be terrifying because you do not know if they are going to kill you or if you will have to kill them in self-defense. Some robbers disguise themselves with a mask, so it could be anybody.

Twists and turns refer to natural disasters. You are sitting on your porch. It a sunny day, but also it is very humid. You feel like there may be some rain in the forecast, so you do not think anything of it. It gets cloudy, so you are thinking that the rain is finally about to come in. Instead of rain, you see a large tornado coming towards your home. You run into the closet and hold the door shut, but you can hear the sound of the tornado approaching you. You hear a "Boom". The tornado has struck the home. You are holding onto the door as tightly as possible. The tornado has finally passed. You open the closet door and immediately you find yourself outside. Your home and everything you owned as has been destroyed.

* * *

Dear Heavenly Father, in the mighty name of Jesus, I come before you in prayer for the reader and their family. Lord, I pray that you keep your people comforted during their times of tragedy. I pray that you restore everything that they may have lost. Lord, I pray that you give them peace. Wrap them in your arms, Jesus. Let them know that all is well. Let them know that there will be glory after this. I speak healing over every illness (mental and physical). Lord, I pray that you keep your people safe in this hour. Please protect them from all hurt, harm, and danger as well as their families. I rebuke the enemy in Jesus name. No weapon formed against them shall prosper. I speak victory. You are an overcomer. In Jesus name, we pray. Amen.

CHAPTER 4: LOOPS

* * *

The loops season is the stagnant season. A loop is a circle. In a circle, you are not going anywhere. You are repeating the same cycle. Imagine riding on a rollercoaster, the ride gets stuck "mid-loop". You are hanging upside down for hours until the ride gets fixed. How uncomfortable would that be? On a normal functioning rollercoaster, the loop part of the ride goes by in a split second. In reality, we can be in a loop for years. These repetitive cycles are called generational curses. Generational curses are a repetition of sin, addictions, and trauma throughout generations. There are times when people carry the weight of their ancestors and never know it.

Loops refer to sexual molestation as a child. The child was molested by her uncle (Mom's brother). The child never told anyone. The child is holding in so much pain. The child feels like it is her fault. The child's mother was also sexually molested by a family member at the age of twelve and got pregnant with her. The mother never told anyone that she was sexually molested. However, it affected the mother's parenting. Her mother is a drug addict to cocaine. The mother and daughter do not communicate well. They do not have a strong bond. The daughter had a stronger relationship with her grandmother because that is who has raised her up until she became a teenager. Her grandmother passed away when she was thirteen. She does not know who her father is. The child feels like she lost the person that loved her most. The daughter then turns to the streets. She is having sex at the age of fourteen with random men for money. She gets pregnant at the age of fifteen. She drops out of school. She is living in and out of the homes of her older friends from the streets.

Loops refer to the results of neglect and abandonment. When a child grows up without a mother or father due to neglect and abandonment, it emotionally and mentally affects a child up unto adulthood. The child is angry, competitive for attention, and feels unloved/unwanted by the people who love them the most. The child has trust issues and is insecure. The child is filled with pride because he/she feels like they don't have any issues and refuses help.

Loops refer to the need for healing and deliverance. We go through so much in a lifetime. Some things we can control and some things we cannot. Generational curses come from the enemy. The enemy wants you to carry that weight of pain forever. We need spiritual deliverance which is freedom from the past. Freedom of whatever haunts you; it can be pain, guilt, shame, anger, rebellion, etc. You can never erase it, but it is important to be free from it so that it no longer affects you negatively. When you are free, you can talk about it without crying or getting angry. You will be able to advise and help with the deliverance of others.

* * *

Dear Heavenly Father, in the mighty name of Jesus, I come before you in prayer for the reader and their family. I rebuke generational curses in this hour. I speak freedom for your people. I speak freedom from their hurtful past. I speak healing and deliverance from their past. I rebuke anger. I pray that your people forgive and forget the things of the past that tries to hold them hostage. I rebuke the enemy right now in Jesus name. Satan, you will let them go. I rebuke strongholds and soul ties, demons that have been living in them for years have to flee. Fill them with your Holy Spirit now. In Jesus name, we pray. Amen.

CHAPTER 5: STRAIGHT

* * *

T he straight season refers to familiarizations of the cycles of life. At this point, you have been through, most of the seasons, if not all. You are very familiar with the curve balls that life throws at you. At the end of any actual rollercoaster ride, you can get off the ride with the anticipation of being able to tell someone else what the ride was like. Once you experience so many things, people will have questions that you will have the knowledge to answer. Your first time getting on a rollercoaster, you have no idea what it is going to be like. When you get off the rollercoaster, you have learned what that experience is like. The goal is to learn from our experiences. The rollercoaster ends going straight. We can get off the rollercoaster with a story/testimony to tell.

Straight refers to being "seasoned" meaning having experienced so much in life that you have become mature as you've been through cycles in your life. You are no longer an amateur or a "rookie". Your first time getting on a roller coaster is normally the most frightening time. The more times you get on rollercoasters,

Daphia Jones Hicks

the more relaxed you are. You already know the do's and the don'ts. You know to make sure you are buckled in, correctly, to not take on loose items, to remain seated until the ride is over, to not eat heavily right before the ride, etc.

Straight refers to being able to minister how God brought you to and through each season. One thing you cannot do is help someone get through something that you never been through. You can tell somebody how God kept you in every season that came your way. God was with you through the good and the bad. You cannot accept the good without also accepting the bad. You have to know that there will be good and bad days. There will be nights when you cry yourselves to sleep. You also have to remember that the things God bring us to, He will also bring us through.

Straight refers to be being fearless because God does not give us the spirit of fear. You can face your trials just as a person faces the fear of riding a rollercoaster for the first time. You can finally say "I can do this" or "I will get through this". You no longer doubt yourself. You are confident in the things you can do. Your faith is so much stronger. Instead of thinking of your obstacles as a death penalty, you will begin to say "I shall live and not die". You will begin to say, "I am more than a conqueror".

* * *

Dear Heavenly Father, in the mighty name of Jesus, I come before you in prayer for the reader and their family. Thank you for delivering your people. Thank you, God, for keeping the minds of your people in their times of trouble. Thank you, God, for never leaving nor forsaking your people. Thank you, God, that through every situation your people have been granted with more wisdom and knowledge. Thank you, God, for the hedge of protection that you have surrounding your people. Lord, we bless you on today and forever. There is no one greater than you. Thank you for being everything we need. Thank you for always coming to see about us when we call your name. Thank you for leading and guiding us. Lord, we pray that you continue to order our steps in your Word. Lord, please strengthen our faith. We can do all things because it is you, Lord, that gives us the strength. Lord, allow your people to remember how they overcame battles before and that they can do it again. Lord, you are the same today, yesterday, and forever. In Jesus name, we pray. Amen.

SCRIPTURES TO REMEMBER DURING THIS LIFE AS A ROLLERCOASTER

Ups

* * *

There once was a man named Job who lived in the land of Uz. He was blameless—a man of complete integrity. He feared God and stayed away from evil. He had seven sons and three daughters. He owned 7,000 sheep, 3,000 camels, 500 teams of oxen, and 500 female donkeys. He also had many servants. He was, in fact, the richest person in that entire area."Job 1:1-3 NLT

"But seek ye first the kingdom of God, and his righteousness; and all these things shall be added unto you."Matthew 6:33 KJV

"And my God will meet all your needs according to the riches of his glory in Christ Jesus."
Philippians 4:19 NIV

Downs

* * *

"I waited patiently for the LORD; And He inclined to me, And heard my cry. He also brought me up out of a horrible pit, Out of the miry clay, And set my feet upon a rock, And established my steps."
Psalms 40:1-2 NKJV

"Cast all your anxiety on him because he cares for you."
1 Peter 5:7 NIV

"Don't worry about anything; instead, pray about everything. Tell God what you need, and thank him for all he has done. Then you will experience God's peace, which exceeds anything we can understand. His peace will guard your hearts and minds as you live in Christ Jesus."
Philippians 4:6-7 NLT

Twists and Turns

* * *

"No weapon formed against you shall prosper, And every tongue which rises against you in judgment You shall condemn. This is the heritage of the servants of the LORD, And their righteousness is from Me," Says the LORD."
Isaiah 54:17 NKJV

"The Lord says, "I will rescue those who love me. I will protect those who trust in my name. When they call on me, I will answer; I will be with them in trouble. I will rescue and honor them."
Psalms 91:14-15 NLT

"But He was wounded for our transgressions, He was bruised for our iniquities; The chastisement for our peace was upon Him, And by His stripes we are healed."
Isaiah 53:5 NKJV

Loops

* * *

So Christ has truly set us free. Now make sure that you stay free, and don't get tied up again in slavery to the law."
Galatians 5:1 NLT

"Therefore submit to God. Resist the devil and he will flee from you."
James 4:7 NKJV

"No temptation has overtaken you except what is common to mankind. And God is faithful; he will not let you be tempted beyond what you can bear. But when you are tempted, he will also provide a way out so that you can endure it."
1 Corinthians 10:13 NIV

Straight

* * *

"For His anger is but for a moment, His favor is for life; Weeping may endure for a night, But joy comes in the morning."
Psalms 30:5 NKJV

"So don't worry about tomorrow, for tomorrow will bring its own worries. Today's trouble is enough for today."
Matthew 6:34 NLT

"But now, O Jacob, listen to the Lord who created you. O Israel, the one who formed you says, "Do not be afraid, for I have ransomed you. I have called you by name; you are mine. When you go through deep waters, I will be with you. When you go through rivers of difficulty, you will not drown. When you walk through the fire of oppression, you will not be burned up; the flames will not consume you."
Isaiah 43:1-2 NLT

ENCOURAGEMENT DURING THIS LIFE AS A ROLLERCOASTER

"I can do this"

* * *

You are standing there looking at a gigantic rollercoaster that is going 110 miles per hour. You are hearing all of the loud screams that fill the entire theme park. Some screams are from thrill while you know others are from fear. You are questioning whether or not you are capable of riding the rollercoaster without fainting. When the ride comes to an end, you see small children getting off of the ride. You say to yourself, "If a 10-year-old can do it, I know I can survive this ride as an adult"

Be inspired and motivated when you see people accomplish the things that you do not feel that you can do. It is okay to be inspired by our youth because God can use anybody including children to motivate you.

"If you go, I'll go"

✻ ✻ ✻

Have you ever been willing to get on a rollercoaster if a friend goes with you? Sometimes we need that support. Whether it is your spouse, your parent, or your best friend, it is great to know that you have someone willing to be by your side during an obstacle. It makes the experience better knowing that you have someone with you.

We cannot get through this life alone. In this world, we need people, especially family and friends. Their encouragement and support are more important to us while we are facing an obstacle or accomplishing a goal than we realize.

"But I'm afraid of heights"

✻ ✻ ✻

As you are standing there looking at that 213ft rollercoaster, you may say "Wow, that is too high for me". Many people are not comfortable going very high in the air. The lower they are to the ground, the more comfortable they feel.

It is the same with going higher in life. The process of going higher can be uncomfortable. We want God to elevate us. In order for God to elevate us, we must face our fears and trust God.

"What's to come"

* * *

Only God knows what is ahead in our future. God is already there but, we have to get there. Our future is already written. God knows every detail of what is in store for us. Many of us want to peek into the next chapter of our lives before we finish the chapter we are in. We must take life day by day. Focus on today.

"This is my first time"

* * *

We have a lot of firsts in our lives. Some of your firsts may include your first time riding a bike without training wheels, first time entering your kindergarten class, first time on an airplane, or even your first time on that humungous rollercoaster. Can you remember how you felt at the moment of your first-time experiences? Pretty anxious? What about nervous? You are not facing anything that has not been faced before. Even though it is your first time, it has been repeated for generations.

You are never facing a first-time experience alone. The first time is a starting point. Remember you have to start before you accomplish or finish your goal.

"The Challenge"

* * *

A challenge is similar to a dare. When someone dares you to do something, they really do not expect you to do it because it is normally something unexpected or outrageous. A challenge is something that people want for you, but some of them will doubt that you will actually get it done. When you are facing a challenge, the pressure is on. Turn the pressure into a plan. For any challenge, you need a plan on how to execute it.

"Buckle down"

* * *

There are 24 hours in a day. It sounds like a long period of time, but in actuality, it goes by fast. You have a list of things that you need to get done. You are questioning your capacity to pull everything off in a timely manner. Begin your day with a prayer and a plan. When you get a plan in place, you have to buckle down in order to get it done.

When you buckle down on a rollercoaster, you cannot get unbuckled until the ride is over. Don't get unbuckled until your tasks are completed today.

"Don't look down"

* * *

In life, we have to keep our head held high. Psalm 121:1 tells us to lift our eyes to the hills. Looking down will only keep you from the blessings that God has for you. Our help comes from looking up to God. God is the only one that can help us. Looking down should never be an option or choice. The enemy wants us to walk around with our head hung low, sad and depressed. The enemy wants us to walk in fear. The devil is a liar. Keep your head held high. Don't get distracted by what is beneath you.

"Incline"

* * *

Most people have a desire to go higher in life. Get a better job, a bigger house, a new car, college degree, etc. All of these things come with challenges and responsibilities. You cannot let those challenges and responsibilities stop you from going higher. If you are not aiming to go higher, you are stagnant. The enemy wants you to be stuck and make zero progress. Even in those challenges, continue to strive for greater.

As the rollercoaster inclines, the last thing you want to happen is for you to get to the very top, and then it rolls backward. The goal is to incline and not decline.

"The Big Drop"

* * *

"The Big Drop" during a rollercoaster ride can be the most exciting and/or frightening part of a person's rollercoaster experience. If you never experienced "The Big Drop", it is when the rollercoaster train slowly creeps to the highest point of the roller-coaster; and the train drops really fast at a steep angle. When we are getting ready to experience something life-changing such as getting married, starting a family, or moving to a new city to start your career; it can be exciting and/or frightening. We want the experience; however, we are ready to get the "The Big Drop" experience over with. Thank God, "The Big Drop" is at the very beginning of an experience and afterward you are more at ease with your journey.

"Stop this ride!"

* * *

Have you ever heard someone screaming to stop the rollercoaster ride after the ride has already started? They are continuously yelling, "Get me off of this thing!" You are thinking to yourself, "That is nonsense. Getting off of a ride while it is still moving equals serious injury or death.

No matter what happens in life we must finish this ride called life on Earth. We cannot end our ride prematurely. We have to wait until the ride comes to an end naturally which is the day God calls us home.

"I want my mommy!"

* * *

Have you ever heard someone scream that they want their mommy on a rollercoaster ride? Was that person possibly you? Parents and guardians can only be with us for a limited amount of time. They cannot be with us for everything, especially as adults. Their job is to prepare us for life after childhood. However, some people do not get the adult preparation that they need.

Once the rollercoaster gets going, you feel like you are alone. Mommy, cannot save you from every situation. In life, we have to remember that Jesus is always there and that we can always call on Him no matter the situation or the time of day or night.

ABOUT THE AUTHOR

My name is Daphia Jones Hicks. I currently reside in Tuscaloosa, Alabama where I was also born and raised. I was born April 9, 1992. I am the youngest sibling with two older sisters. I obtained a BS in Psychology at the University of Phoenix. I have been married to my husband for four years. I have one son; he is two years of age. I am a Minister at my local church. I have been in ministry for two years. I have a Women's Ministry called Empowered Women in Christ and a Prayer/Intercessory Ministry called Keep Prayer Alive. God has done so much and brought me so far in such a small period of time. God truly has His hand upon my life. The favor of God is upon me. I am so humble because I know that I would not be where I am if it had not been for God's grace and mercy. I pray that each of you continue to follow me on this journey. You can follow me on Facebook to hear about my upcoming books and events. Facebook: Min Daphia Hicks.

Made in the USA
Columbia, SC
11 May 2021